Praise for *I Remember*

These are the stories of a 'king-sized' life, one of my favorite poems in this collection—Mary Helms' second book of poetry. Sensuous—it bright with the sounds of voices, present with scents wafting in from orchards, up from cellars, out of homes once known. A song of joy for things lost and life found, the immutable evidence of the powerful bonds of love that continue to triumph—*Even in our brokenness, our tree bore luscious, hardy fruit.*

Sally Uhler Boswell

Mary's gift has arrived for all to enjoy! In her new book of poetry, she shares a lifetime of treasured memories that, until now, have been softly locked in her heart. We meet her family and friends through the complexities of relationship—of love, loss and letting go. As the threads of life are woven into caring and quiet bonding, she reminds us that we must enjoy the moment because the breaking of a single thread creates deep sadness and vulnerability.

Our senses are stimulated by the fragrance of buttercups, the aroma of pickles and preserves and Saturday's simmering vegetable soup. Sounds, songs, and voices cause us to hum and become wrapped in a long-forgotten melody of our own. We are touched by the innocence of a small child's need to protect an ailing parent. Our mind's eye envisions the protective canopy of trees planted long ago. We experience the sensation of free fall when trust and risk struggle against the need for control and safety. The eyes of owlets give us a glimpse of strong faith and devotion. Hopscotching travels around the globe welcome new experiences, reflection, joy, and laughter. We feel Mary's quiet peace and warm love through every word she writes.

Joann Burstein

I was deeply gifted by Mary's words, her sacred Spirit, her memories and moved to explore my own history, moved to grieve and feel the pain and gift of grief. Moved to listen for the birds outside my office door. Moved to go look at old photographs of family and places and smells that are not forgotten.

I am grateful.

Thomas Ledbetter

Also by Mary Helms

lost and found, and other poems of loss, grief, and joy

I Remember

a poetic memoir

Mary Helms

Copyright © 2019 by Mary Helms

ISBN: 978-0-578-49226-1
First Edition

All rights reserved under International and Pan-American Copyright Conventions. No part of this book may be reproduced in any manner whatsoever without written permission from the copyright holder, except in the case of brief quotations embodied in critical articles and reviews.

Cover Photos: From Mary Helms' photo collection
Cover Design & Interior Layout: Crystal Heidel, Byzantium Sky Press, LLC

Printed in the USA

Dear Reader,

This book of poems is my second. In my first, I wrote these words to you:

> If I made a list years ago of 100 things in my future, ALS would not have made the list, but the list would have been made with the assumption of a loving God who has good things in store for me. I am still guided by that faith, believing that all circumstances contain gifts. I want to recognize and receive them. That is not an easy task at times, and the process often involves deep grief as well as joy.

The favorable response to *lost and found, and other poems of loss, grief and love* continues to energize me and motivated me to publish the poems in this book. These are older and new poems that reach beyond the very specific observations, emotions and insights of my ALS experience, to create a memoir, a more complete poetic memoir.

As I reflect upon all of my poems, a powerful deeply embedded message in my human psyche emerges: Life is cumulative.

Now is indeed the sum of all the good and the positive in my life, along with the bad and negative. My poems—as I write them, read them, hear them read aloud—enable me to be aware of this precious Now.

When I live in the moment, as I do, I know this as one of the very good things that God continues to have in store for me.

Thank you, Dear Reader.

Mary Helms

I dedicate this memoir in poetry to my grandchildren:

Katherine, Christine, Daniel,

Christopher, Tanner, Phillip,

Caroline, Eva, Althea

Thanks to all who read my poems aloud so I could hear their sound. Each encouraged and inspired me to write more. A special thanks to Ellen Collins, my teacher who first let me know I had a message and patiently showed how to express it and to my partner, George Beckerman, who was there for me every step of the way.

CONTENTS

FOREWORD iii

CHILDHOOD

Visiting the Old House 3
Dear Mama.. 4
Pickles and Preserves... 5
A Lifetime.. 6
Summer Nights.. 8
Money Talk.. 9
The Old Bank 10
The Truth 11
Jobs 12
Wishful..13
Even in August 14
About Jane..15
Leaving the House Where My Grandmother Had Lived 16
Lost Childhood...17

TRAVEL

From Africa 21
In Mexico 22
Italian Lemon 23
Recovery..24
Joy Train..25
Red Phone Booth 26
To England..27
Vietnam Defined My Outer Edges 28

MY LATER LIFE

Not Billy Collins...31
Stranger.. 32
Before the Moving Van... 33
The Friendship of Women.. 34
Free Fall 35

Hello, Beauty	36
Hands	37
Mama in Nature	38
Wedding Day	39
Finding a Voice	40
King-sized	41
My Man	42
April Pain	43
At Gary's Grave	44
At St. Peter's	45
Waves	46
A Cloud of Butterflies	47
Having Choices	48
Last Words	49
After Elizabeth Barrett Browning	50
Blue Chair	51
The Next Place	52
Brief Glimpse of Light	53
Life Bonds	54
Deep Practice	55
Hair	56
Holy Eyes	57
Missing Home	58
My Call	59
Quiet Love	60
The Doll	61
The Flirt	62
To Althea	63
The Blessing	64
Communion	65
Notes Not Yet Sounded	66

FOREWORD

Thank goodness Mary Helms is offering us a second book of poems to follow *lost and found*.

I am pleased to have Mary's books on my shelf for whenever I need to hear her solid voice and find peace.

Despite her challenge of ALS, and being unable to speak for herself, we still always have her published voice available to us.

Each one of us has our own voice. Mary's voice is especially valuable as it gives us peacefulness in a noisy world. She offers us a good way to look at our own lives. We learn from her wisdom. I hear and feel Mary's voice as calm, stable, quiet, sensible, matter-of-fact, truthful, steady. Especially, peaceful.

For information on The ALS Association Greater Philadelphia Chapter, go to www.alsphiladelphia.org.

Elizabeth Stoner

CHILDHOOD

Visiting the Old House

From a distance the old house on the hill
looked the same, unchanged in twenty years.
It might still hold a trace of memory,
and my childhood would not be gone after all.
I might find the secret room, small and bright,
even one of my grandmother's chipped cups, stained,
now holding green cuttings,
paintbrushes in turpentine, papers tied together with string,
and Emily Dickinson's poems marked in the margins.
But I knew the moment I entered,
even though I came in the back door,
one kept and painted by the new owner,
that all was gone.

Dear Mama

Mama, I am seeing you in my dreams,
busy in your backyard,
trying to clean the jumble in the garage,
wanting to make sense of life.
I try to call you to let you know I'm coming for supper,
but my phone is too small.

Remember the many times we walked
from bed to bed talking about your flowers,
the azaleas, white and red,
and volunteer pale petunias?
Are you coming to my bed in the night
for one more conversation?

You come into my mind in daytime, too,
late afternoon, the time I usually called.
Oh Mama, what binds us even now?
Is it my regret that I didn't know
what it was to be like you?
Or do I know so well
that the moths of memory
hold us as one?

Pickles and Preserves

The hot water pipe in the kitchen sprung a leak yesterday,
so the handyman was handy and he took a look around.
"I'll have you fixed in no time," he said,
and fixed he did, knocking down a shelf of jars
full of pickles and preserves in the cellar
right after he fixed the pipe.
And what was I to do but go below into the mess
with my broom and dust pan,
buckets of water and scrub brush?
When I finished the job the aroma of pickles and preserves
was all around me and stayed on my hands and hair.
When I went to the store, the check-out lady sniffed,
but I paid her no mind.

The cat woke me at 4:00 a.m. this morning and there was no more sleep.
The mockingbird was singing his love song to his mate already
and I heard a Bob White not far away.
In Virginia in summer the sky is pink early,
so I go outside in the cool, before the heavy heat
creeps around in the shade of the backyard trees
and yesterday's smells rise again
like pickles and preserves.

A Lifetime

My hands were beautiful when I was twelve,
against the small tablecloth for Mom's bridge table.
A blue cloth, the quiet dense blue
of the small Wedgwood pitcher in the corner cupboard.
The ladies had finished playing bridge
and it was time for the chocolate cake Mom had made
to share a spot on the dessert plate with a mound of vanilla ice cream.
"Mary Eleanor, you have beautiful hands."
It was Mrs. Campbell, Mom's friend.
"Your hands are such a nice shape and look so perfect
against the blue of the cloth."
I looked at my hands,
seeing them for the first time,
seeing them as a part of me that was perfectly formed,
seeing myself as beautiful.

Years later when one of my grandchildren touched the back of my hand,
smoothing the wrinkled skin,
pressing lightly against the veins, pale blue,
I began to feel beauty in a new way.
Her fingers reminded me of touching my grandmother.
Her hands were warm and relaxed.
I pulled little tents of skin on the back of her hand
and let them go slowly back to the flatness,
freckled with spots the color of biscuits
just out of the oven.
She let me turn her hand over
and my finger traced the lines of her palm.
A small rough spot near the base of her pointer
stopped my finger for a moment.
I rubbed it a bit
and then I kissed it.
Somehow I knew that I could make that little spot well
with my mouth.

Grandma made a soft sound,
almost a hum.
Now I can feel her hum in myself.
I know her in me.

Beautiful.

Summer Nights

There was a glider on the porch of my childhood,
and I slept there on the hottest of Virginia nights,
nightgown stuck to my sweaty back
and pillow catching the heat of my face.
My little sister was on the daybed,
on the side of the porch with no breeze,
and in the still air, she quieted and fell asleep.
If I wiggled even a bit, the glider moved
and squeaked, reminding me of the day.
My mother sang, "You are my sunshine."
Her voice cooled the night air
and was the last small sound I heard.

Money Talk

It was hot,
and when we got to my grandma's house
it was even hotter.
We went to the cool cellar
where she had already put the church money,
canvas bags of coins and bills.
The coins came tumbling out on the table
set square in the middle of the room.
She let me make stacks: quarters, dimes, nickels, and pennies,
and she talked all the while we were stacking.
The sound of her voice was a little push and crackle.
Natural.
It came out of her mouth natural.
She just said whatever she thought.
She didn't have to hold back like I did with others,
so I didn't hold back either.
And the sound and smell and taste of the talk
was easy
and spicy.

The Old Bank

The old bank building is a flower shop now,
and the new bank,
impressively large with grounds
that befit a southern estate,
doesn't invite me the way the old bank did.
There everyone knew my name,
even though I was only twelve
and the cash I had to deposit after my birthday
was only six dollars because I had spent four
at the five-and-dime across the street.

When I return for a visit now,
I go into the flower shop,
smell the gardenias,
touch the front of a Norfolk Island Pine,
taking the time to remember
my dark blue pass book
before I purchase
a small bunch of white daisies.

The Truth

My father was a truthful man,
spending his deceit on little lies
that let us see his flaws
and love him more for them.

He would say, "I haven't had a bowl of ice cream in years."
It was true because he usually ate ice cream right out of the carton,
standing in front of the refrigerator with the freezer door open.
Chocolate was his favorite.
When he ate vanilla,
it was with a piece of apple pie
or beside a slice of yellow cake with chocolate icing.
And somehow they never came out even
so another scoop of ice cream was required.

When he dozed during the sermon,
sitting in the front row
in the short pew that was handy,
it was because he had total confidence in the preacher,
or so he said.

I share his attitude about ice cream.
I learned from him
when we had secret Popsicles before supper,
a time that might spoil our appetites.
It never did.
But I keep my eyes open in church.
That's where big lies can fly
and I want to catch them
if they do.

Jobs

I went out to the cucumber shed early,
before the farmers had brought
big canvas bag of cucumbers
to be sorted,
before the sorting machines had lumbered
into noisy action,
before my father's men had arrived
to shove bushel baskets
at the end of the long conveyor belts
to catch the cucumbers in sorted sizes.

The big open shed was quiet
and sunlight sprayed rays of still dust,
something like the afternoon sun
came through the stained-glass windows
of the church up the hill.

I walked past the stacked baskets
waiting for their job,
toward a gray cat sitting,
washing his face with his paw,
but he hurried to work.
Catching mice was his job.

Wishful

Oyster stew for breakfast every Christmas morning.
Did we really have it
or was it something I so desired
that I created the memory?
Like the warm scent of my father
when he hugged me close
and the perfect vegetable soup simmering
on Saturdays
and my mother humming?
Even a childhood full of comfort
has small dark spots.

I fill my empty places with stories
of pleasure
to add to the story
I invent as I grow old.
I hold on tightly
as my hybrid creation
means more,
lifts me from original roots.

Even in August

My father sick, flushed with high fever,
with a smell like no other, strong,
as if he were fighting by throwing off heat.
His large body seems even larger when he lies down.
He makes muttering noises and heaves a wave of sighs.
I sit on the small hassock close to the head of his bed
to talk to him a bit.

"Can I get you anything, Daddy?"
"Water," his reply.
He drinks from the tall glass.
A groan.
I sit here as he dozes, a swell of heat rising from his body.
The chills will come, I know, and he will shudder,
helpless.
He has no defense.
Blankets piled high, even in August, are not enough
to forbid the cold fire that poisons him.
Someday he will die, but this time
I sit close to his head.
Guarding him.

About Jane

My sister was born five days before my second birthday.
I don't remember, of course, but I can't imagine
a day without her.
We sat together on our grandmother's green Adirondack chair
and ate strawberry ice cream.
We chased her cat
and played hide and seek in her yard,
hiding our eyes against the trunk of the catalpa tree.
In later years, when it was house-selling time,
we walked around the yard and picked up pecans
just as she had done years before.
We told each other stories,
wove new memories out of old ones,
and shared shadows of reflection.
We talked about what we knew about those gone before us,
what we thought we knew, what we wondered about.
We read from faded letters and newspaper articles,
washed chipped china plates and cups,
found mysterious keys and bifocal spectacles,
rummaged through old trunks,
sorting out feelings as we sorted covers and quilts.
Now we vow to finish all old business
and toss our junk before we die,
so our children won't have the chore.
I know that vow will be broken,
for our life is lived with the legacy of memories,
and some who bear resemblance
will carry them one more time.

Leaving the House Where My Grandmother Had Lived

I was stopped by the sight of buttercups,
strewn wildly and wide on the edge of the yard,
that place where we had stood so often,
looking at the far expanse of the fields in spring
when they had been plowed in expectant rows,
and she would tell me if this was the year for soybeans,
or corn, or the land to rest and wait for winter wheat.
And the buttercups,
how many times she held one under my willing chin
to learn if I was made of butter!
Oh grandmother of my sweetest memories,
poised still to hold me
and tell me what I am made of,
I am made of you.

Lost Childhood

I heard their voices at night
and the reassuring sound lulled me to sleep.
My father's voice, sure and warm, and my mother's,
curled comfortably around his,
much like the way he curved his arm
around her waist in the kitchen before supper,
when the smell of bread, almost done,
aroused his hunger.

Years later, the sharp sound of their quarrel
from the yard comes to my open window.
A summer morning.
While an oriole whistles his song,
I listen and feel my childhood slip away.

TRAVEL

From Africa

I listen to my yoga breath,
the sound
like the first sound
in my mother's womb,
the sound
heard by the Masai baby
in her mother's womb.
We are kin.

Be careful what you ask me,
I may tell you more than you want to know.
The Spirit is moving round the globe.

Be careful what you ask me,
I may tell you about girls
with bodies injured by childbirth,
children themselves, shamed,
about newborn babies baptized quickly
before they die,
mothers in resignation rather than joy.
Do I tell you more than you want to know?

The Spirit has moved into my chest.
A mother quivers on a hospital bed,
twins dead,
next to the mother who smiles at her newborn boy.

The Spirit has moved into my throat.
Do I tell you about them or me?
Does this come from their pelvis or mine,
from my pain or theirs?
Are we separate or one?
I may answer with questions.

In Mexico

79 years old and wearing a floaty white embroidered smock,
so different from the sensible tailored shirts
I usually choose.
I'm showing off a part of myself
full of silliness and joy.
Tonight, the last night of a vacation in Mexio,
I'm celebrating being me,
grateful for the discovery of parts of myself
that lumbered in the world of work,
responsible decision making, and staying on the path.
No regrets or paths not chosen.
And tonight I show off and love myself.

Italian Lemon

He stood in the market in Rome,
the one near the Spanish Steps.
His eyes, dark, captured mine,
and his mouth promised a thousand kisses
before he walked my way,
a lemon in his hand.
He touched me, on my arm
below my elbow, a place of my strong pulse
and disappeared.

Recovery

I sink back in the bathtub bubbles
and my toes, funny and pink, pop up.
Can these be mine?
I feel so tired, like I've had a day of hiking hills
rather than barely making it up the stairs.
My toes are a wonder,
wiggling,
telling their story in mime.
"We are here," they say, "and we want to have fun!
Knees and shoulders are more worn than we,
so give them a soak.
We'll wait. Let us take the lead."
I did.
Now I'm ready, with my hearing aid,
foolish dangles,
and my flat party shoes with shiny toes.

Joy Train

The East Midlands train to Sheffield
brings me to a joyful snort as I scurry along the platform,
anticipating a sunny ride in First Class,
trusting the English sky.
Past blocks of sturdy houses and square automobiles,
the window fills with sudden green.
Hedgerows of hawthorns, showing white cascades,
hiding cruel thorns while promising the birds red berries,
the horse chestnut trees, wild and willowy, flinging white tassels,
and the fading white lust of wild cherry trees
stand in the distance like an *a capella* choir,
full-throated on first note, gloriously in tune.

Red Phone Booth

Past Nag's Head Inn on Loxley Road,
where Friday's special
is steak and Stilton and ale with pork pies,
and the old men are at the pool table by noon,
cues extended with low-bellied stretches,
a red phone booth stands still,
far past its time.
The redness faded and crackled
like the skin of the oldest sage,
beautifully weathered,
moss on its lower ridges,
a snail shell in a corner wedge.
I stand in awe.
Even now for those strong enough
to pull the door open,
a call is possible from this place.
With this old friend I can call Singapore,
or Sparta, or the Nag's Head Inn.

And so with me,
though I cannot speak as I could once,
some old friend or curious child
is strong enough to listen
and hear my voice.

To England

Your roses were not ready when I came in early May,
and daffodils were spent,
but black tulips rose round the corners of Regent Park,
and in Rosabel's small garden,
crimson peonies flopped their huge heads
near the kitchen door.
Bluebells spread as far as I could see
on Sunday's stroll in the valley,
and by the red phone booth on the corner of Stacey Lane,
a giant dandelion with five yellow faces
showed her wild self.

Vietnam Defined My Outer Edges

The strangeness of the toilets,
a street corner feast of chicken and rice,
night markets, lit with torches in Dalat,
the color and sound of women's voices.
I crossed the street in Saigon.
walking a diagonal, steady pace,
trusting the rhythm of bicycles and trucks.

Children in villages cluster around us,
eager for our cameras to remember their smiles.
Once we met an old woman on a narrow bridge
whose face told stories of a thousand years.
No camera could capture this memory.

MY LATER LIFE

Not Billy Collins

My lover read a Billy Collins poem to me.
The words were delicious in his mouth
and almost licked the rim of my ear,
giving me a shiver of sadness mixed with delight,
knowing I will never be able to write such a perfect poem,
never, even if I write for a hundred days.
But my imperfect lines are enough
to keep me going,
for as words come to me,
I pause,
I open,
I fill my place.
I write my poems for they are only mine to write.
I fly low along the coast with the ocean on one side
and the setting sun on the other,
all in my time.

Stranger

Who is the old woman in the photo?
White hair and creviced mouth,
little lines like my mother's,
she is with my son and has a scarf like mine,
but I don't know her.
An uninvited guest.
I'll try to be kind to her,
I know I should.
Perhaps we will take slow walks together,
taking time to talk about the flowers we see on the way.

I wonder if she plays bridge.

Before the Moving Van

Leaving will happen soon enough,
with boxes to pack and the tools of daily life to sort,
but not yet.
Let me spend the morning
staying,
remembering,
seeing.
I sit in the old rocker in the corner of the dining room
and take it in.
Each window holds an image, living art,
and the clerestory window releases my eye to sky
and treetops that tremble and tip in the wind.
There on the far wall, a painting
that hung over my mother's sofa for forty years,
so that when she died
she came with me in this frame.
The painting, cleaned of the years of grime
from living with her wood stove,
joined my days and nights.
This room, so full of sun and movement and memories,
tells me of myself, of my yearning
to create and connect.
This space of high ceiling and generous light,
lives green inside and out,
holds old and new.
On a table, a photograph of my children
all younger than five,
another of their children,
and my grandmother's compote.
It's all there on one table,
in one place,
my heart.

The Friendship of Women

Three busy women, often with time booked,
we are free for each other at the same time.
We weekend together,
cups of coffee, wine in new glasses,
time on the porch in white wicker chairs,
close enough to talk low-voiced,
sad and silly and seldom heard,
our voices touch,
a special cadence,
a way of joining hands over the years.
A photograph of four reminds us
we are vulnerable,
and brings us
to silence.

Free Fall

In the circus show I can hardly bear
to watch the trapeze artists,
swinging,
        letting go,
               catching each other,
                      being caught.
Surely even knowing there is a safety net
would not be enough for me to let go,
let go,
let go,
to trust that another will catch me.

Better to fall into the net than to trust the other.

Deep within me is a voice…no, a sound.
It comes in a spasm in my belly and quickens my breath.
There it is now…..I feel it in my chest, bigger than my chest,
so big I have to sit up straight to give it room.
I want to stay in my head.
I know that place.
It is safe and familiar and in control.
I see myself on the trapeze,
up to my old tricks.

Hello, Beauty

I see you with my mind and heart as well as my eyes.
Last night my son played a video from twenty years ago
and I saw you in my sleeping grandson,
his perfect nose and mouth, the silence of him.

I see you when I give you time to show.
I judged my mother funny, irritating,
outrageous at times.
Now her photograph moves me to tears, longing.

I see you in the red feather on my window sill.
A friend sent it to me on my birthday
from the tail of his 34 year old African Gray.
You are old and young and rich with love.

I see you when I close my eyes
and listen for the sound of my lover.
He calls my name when he comes in the house
and says it once more when he enters the room.

I saw you in the first light of today
filtered through the curtain
soft at the window by my bed.
You waited for me, it seemed, to come awake.

Hello, Beauty.

Hands

Hail to you, Mistress of Marriott Bedmaking!
You overcome vomit, semen, and shit,
battle blood, shoe polish, and disregard.
Your name is housekeeper,
and you welcome me away from home.

Smooth white sheets ensure my rest,
a light coverlet envelops me with warmth,
so I feel as safe as I did
when my mother tucked me in with a kiss,
and held my folded hands as I said my prayers,
asking God's blessing on all I knew.
Plumped pillows give me support
for my bedtime iPad Solitaire
and journaling to store today's reflection
and hopes that tomorrow will come,
and when I turn off the light,
one pillow, just right for my weary head
will lead me to sleep.

Your hands
are of a color darker than mine,
have a story to tell that I will not know.

Accept my feeble attempt to express gratitude
for your kind and dutiful preparation
by leaving a tip.
Your hands
may love the feel of cash,
and I leave it carefully folded,
so you will know my folding hands
and yours have met
in serving each other.

Mama in Nature

When Mama's body was taken from the house,
the pain
seized me like a great black bear,
sudden,
totally gripping me,
then tearing out my gut,
claws spread to eat my tender places.
A creature of nature doing what it knows to do.

I roared my grief,
a primal reply.
Yet I was far from some great wilderness and wildness.
I sat in the room where she had slept,
I fit into her favorite chair,
its worn arms holding me.
I wept.
A creature of nature
doing what I know to do.

Wedding Day

The bride's mother has photos of the wedding party,
the attendants of the bride
in pink dresses and hats and cheeks, and never mind
that the maid of honor was too tall
and the best man too short.
Chantilly lace over taffeta with a bouquet of orchids,
perfection for the bride,
and if the soloist was slightly off key,
no one noticed.
Certainly not me.
It was "I do" and "will obey,"
baskets of gladiola and tradition,
and Grandma nodded in approval.
Rain brought flurries of panic
as it came over the hill straight to the gardens
where rows of draped tables waited like maiden aunts,
laden with small cakes, layered and iced,
tiny triangles, and dreams.
Guests flocked into the house,
milling in polite confusion,
wondering where to find a dry receiving line.
Soon laughter exploded in the delight of relatives from far away,
old-fashioned friendships of children and grandfather,
neighbors finding places for napkins, nuts, and mints
on tables moved at top speed for shelter.
No one cried,
certainly not the groom or bride.
As they came out ready for their departure,
so much rice it looked like snow,
and the guests could have stocked the newlywed pantry
for rice pudding.
But cooking
was on no one's mind.

Finding a Voice

When I felt no one was listening
I went to a place so quiet
that even a whisper sounded
louder than the space could hold.
Once I felt so unheard I changed my life.
I yelled, wept with despair.
Desperate at being unknown,
I left my marriage.

I remember a moment
raking leaves on an autumn day.
The rhythm of the raking,
the sound of the leaves
as they shuffled against each other
and the tines of the rake
were like conversation.

I had no companion, in my deepest part.
Even the daily tending of my life
was clouded in gray silence.
On that day I heard a voice
I didn't know was mine.
I began to listen.
A voice still learning to speak,
even now.

King-sized

I love changing the sheets on our bed,
smooth, smooth, smoothing the white expanse
with my hands spread wide,
and tucking the corners tight
just as my mother taught me.

We did not conceive a child in this bed,
we conceived a life,
gathering our dreads and dreams,
sounds of love and sleep,
pillows propped with possibilities.

We have a king-sized life.

My Man

He sits before the big window, writing,
and I love the look of him,
his white hair needing a trim,
his favorite shirt, shabby with comfort,
the collar against his ear.
He turns when he hears me.
The sun is out this morning, he says,
and I know it in his face.

April Pain

Her dismay,
like April rain that turns
in a moment to sleet,
breaking buds on trees
and ruining the peaches of the season,
stayed on her face for a lifetime.
Even when she smiled, a faint frown at the corner of her mouth
told the story
of how the hurt lingered
like a small black pearl.
No one knew her pain,
discreetly nurtured,
spoiled fruit.

At Gary's Grave

I didn't expect the hole to be so deep.
I had never looked into a grave before,
deep, deeper than I expected.
Down in the dark space of no hope,
dirt hits the coffin,
a startling sound.
Beside the grave,
his mother cries,
and cries more,
sobbing sounds
that catch her chested heart
and pull it through her throat,
the throat that sang his infant songs
and called to him across the football field.

I didn't expect the hole
to be so deep.

At St. Peter's

I am working on pride,
the sin most obvious,
and yesterday I saw a symbol
that moved me.
The young Episcopal head bowed,
her dark hair following the move of her face,
white vestments, plain.

I know the practice of bowing
is not one I own.
I yearned for it in that moment of beautiful obedience.
With that act, my body joins my heart and mind
and becomes holy learning for me.

Waves

I waved,
holding on to each one as long as I could,
as if the lift of my hand
and flutter of my fingers
could make time stay still,
and we would not say good-bye.

Some left under the slender moon,
most in the bright light of day,
and I could see them waving
down the driveway,
around the corner.
We waved as if our hands were speaking,
saying words of love,
regret,
promises to return.

A Cloud of Butterflies

What is my voice? I wonder,
who is my voice?
Which of the many me's will speak
for the me I want to reveal?
Sensible, logical, whimsical, passionate me.
Glorious, frightened, confused me,
giddy as a butterfly,
a cloud of butterflies
fluttering in a patch of spring.
Stilted me, unvoiced for years but still convinced
I have something to say.
Silent me, waiting.
Sad me, wishing.
Silly me warbling like a bird
hopping over her eggy nest.
Seventy-one year me,
still waiting to come out.

Having Choices

Sunday morning and a choice,
church, lingering breakfast and newspaper,
or walking with sunshine for the first time in a long time.
I am stopped by this notion of choice
and remember the safe days I knew
where I would be, on the hard bench near the front on the right side.
I'd look across the church and see my grandmother
and my aunt wearing her tan all-weather coat
and the scarf she bought in Paris.
Mom would be at the organ and Dad in the front row,
and if he nodded off during the sermon,
that was just a vote of confidence in the preacher, he'd say.
The rustle of church bulletins and church voices,
hello whispers and clearing of throats for the first hymn.
Week after week, year after year.
I had no idea what a year meant then.
I couldn't picture myself on Sunday morning
older than my grandmother, older than any of my living kin,
having choices.

Last Words

There was no casket at the funeral, not even an urn of ashes.
Martha would not want us reminded of her death,
how she slipped away in the gray silent time before dawn.
So the candles, everyone lit a candle as if it were Christmas Eve
and time to sing "Silent Night."
When we sang "Somewhere Over the Rainbow,"
I didn't think of Judy Garland for a minute.
My voice followed the others to fly high with the blue birds
and promised to believe that I could.

Elizabeth, my aunt, died as I sat beside her,
waiting her turn.
She planned her own funeral years before,
giving instructions to the minister more than once.
She wanted "Amazing Grace" and Psalm 23
and no one chewing gum.
We walked with the casket to the place she reserved
beside her mother.
She had told me in her eighty-ninth year,
"I still miss Mama."

How do you live a life and say good-bye?
Will I miss my mother's voice near the close of my days
or wonder how the blue birds fly?

After Elizabeth Barrett Browning

How does he love me?

By saying goodbye three times
  before he leaves our house
by rolling over in the night
  and reaching for my hand,
by giving me endless choices for dinner
  and eating leftovers at home,
by reminding me to water the plants
  though he knows I don't need reminding,
by sitting with me in silence,
  just because,
by talking on and on
  as long as I will listen,
by touching my hair,
  my cheeks, my mouth,
by being anxious,
  by being reassuring
by mail, text, and notes on the kitchen counter.

Blue Chair

I miss my blue chair,
winged back, comfortable, a safe blue.
I bought it for my special kitchen corner,
where I had a clear view of the brick patio,
forsythia and dogwood in the spring,
the spread of yarrow, cherry tomatoes,
cleome, tiger lilies, and pink petunias in summer,
and a cascade of sweet autumn clematis
over the fence in fall.
I found a small wicker table
in a thrift shop, painted a faded blue.
It quietly took its place for my journal,
the newspaper, the occasional note from my son
far away in New Zealand.
I learned my need for quiet in the blue chair,
and took it with me to other corners,
other chairs, other gardens.

The Next Place

I grieve the losses, all of them.
My father, as he lay heavy and hot to my touch,
called me to a time of memory and more.
My mother, I listened to her breath as it slowed,
took less space in her breast, and broke my heart.
A house so close to ocean waves I could hear their sound
when I woke before the sun rose,
a walnut tree planted by a bride a hundred years before,
now worn out by worms and insulted by the power saw,
my arthritic knees, all the hikes not taken, and tennis shots not made.
And now my quick remark and my hearty smile have left
tiny lines of age and drought for my eye in the mirror.

I grieve these losses, losing and letting go,
orphaned, sobered by my own reflection, silent.
I want to go on to the far place
that calls me to be who I might be,
and return to forgotten stars in my early sky
to write poetry and prayers.

Brief Glimpse of Light

I saw him in the elevator,
black, his lively hair in a twisted crown,
and I saw his nose from the side,
dark and nostril-wide and wondrously his.
In that moment I knew him as a soul, a person,
an energy who had existed before he had hair or nose.
I knew how we as souls might have been surprised
by how we were housed and woke up our first day.
We had no choice.
We woke up to discover what we were on our outside,
our shell, our cover for this life.
As infants we shuddered without the womb,
looked at our baby hands in wonder,
heard our own cries in amazement.
And moment by moment
we forgot who we were,
captured by what others saw and heard.
And who I was and am and will be
come to me in a brief glimpse
of light in an elevator.

Life Bonds

We'd been divorced many years when he died,
and I was surprised by my tears.
My seventeen-year-old heart broke open
and I wept
for the young passion that drove us
into each other's arms without reserve.

We shared our young unknowing,
and there were magic days
when we walked holding hands
with another, and two and three and four,
whose small hands
were more than we could hold.
Even in our brokenness,
our tree bore luscious hardy fruit.

Now in the midst of family,
I walk a solitary path of memory,
for only he knew my hungry innocence,
the way I rose at night to hear
his whispered longing,
touched and smelled his skin.
Bonded, we are lost together.

Deep Practice

Deep down inside I want that love that completely overpowers me,
that fills me with such joy
I cannot hold the sweet moisture that comes
and flows and overflows.
I swell with life as I imagine the moment
I see him after our first night of lovemaking,
when he shows up at my door in daylight
and I step toward him
with my mind and body and heart.
It is a holy moment.
I know it now as I write it…
as I name it…
as I recognize it as my god self,
stepping totally into life.
It gives me practice,
lets me know I want to step into death,
conscious, moving, stepping toward Him,
stepping toward God who has been waiting
all this time.

Hair

What is it about hair that makes us smile and frown?
It seduces our fingers, and twirling strands of curls
arouses lust and longing and promises.
I saw a young man touch his love's long hair casually,
as if she would not notice his need, his adoring fingers
tracing the patterns learned
as he rested on his mother's shoulder long ago,
and I imagined his son doing the same
in some far time.

Holy Eyes

You have let the owl lay eggs
in a dark and hidden high place
and when the owlets looked over the rim,
you showed them to me.
Look up, You must have said,
otherwise how would I have known
that the sweet row of bright eyes would be
visible in the last light of dusk?
You know all, and Your knowing
lifts my eyes to a holy place.
How Holy are You,
am I,
in the eyes of the owlets!

Missing Home

I know myself today,
bereft without the trees of home,
the shade canopy of the yard when the sun comes up and over,
before its light penetrates the deeply leafed chestnut trees, the poplars,
whose names were spoken to me by my mother and my father's mother,
all women who have known and spoken of trees and sunrise and silence.
Understand what it means to me
to lose my place,
to lose the place where whippoorwill and deer and worms and lichen
live,
to lose the place of my heart,
where the canopy held me,
protected me,
invites me still.

My Call

O Holy One, I awake each morning hungry for You,
for your presence in me and around me.
I call You...
O Holy One,
O Holy One,
Dear God,
Precious Spirit,
Sweet Wind of my Soul,
Hey Jesus,
Mother God,
Merciful Father,
All Knowing One,
Loud Voice,
Burning Bush,
Lover of my soul,
Oh God,
Heavenly Father.

You have more names than I have words
to describe
or call You.
I know You are here.
You show up as soon as I call.
You show up before I call.
You are in the roaring in my ears,
the little crack sound in my neck.
You know my body better than I...
You made it.
Still.
Waiting.
I am still.
I need call no more.

Quiet Love

You turn your head to the side,
considering what you will say.
In that brief moment you travel
to a place of exotic recall
hearing a faint sound.
And when you turn your face to mine,
I see the slight shadow
of a dark street in Budapest
which called to you years go.
Your voice seems an echo
and I know you have not returned.

I loved you from the first moment
you spoke to me,
like opening a love letter in French,
not reading a word, but knowing it all.
You knew how to cradle my head,
knew as if you had waited for me your whole life.
Now I wait for your return
in a quiet space.

The Doll

Broken, I stand silent among the chatter.
And yet a child wants me,
holds me in kinship, for she is silent too.
She knows my secret language,
dreams my scattered dreams
held in a misty shawl.
We walk a sacred pathway,
her arms around my waist.
Held by her, I am whole.

The Flirt

So here's to April!
She must be a girl month.
Only a girl month could be so temperamental,
flirty weather, sunshine and snow.
She peeks through tulip
and falls from forsythia,
laughing at our confusion.

"Don't be so stuffy!" she says.
"It matters not if you wear wool or cotton,
short sleeve or long,
sweater or shawl!
Whatever you choose will simply suit for a moment,
and then the moment will slip away!
May and June will show up soon
and leave you longing."

To Althea

Youngest grandchild of mine,
you have a place in my heart like no other,
for you were the latest infant held in my arms.
Your face and body were beautifully unique,
and still I saw the likeness of your kin.
Your place in the world is yours to fill
with ideas, kindness, and your own imagination.
Hooray for Althea, poet, painter, scientist, scholar,
and girl of flowers.

The Blessing

There was a moment that was beyond my understanding.
The feeling in my chest was so big my body couldn't hold it.
I looked into his eyes, this new person in my arms,
and wondered how he was there with me in this moment
and how I could have carried him in my body all those months
without knowing his name,
without knowing his need,
without knowing his helpless power over me.
I hadn't expected him to be red and wrinkled
and his hands so small.
I didn't know he would have this black hair and flat nose.
His eyes were scrunched into two tiny lines.
Then he changed.
The little lines broke open and his eyes,
blue and clear, conquered me,
took hold of my fear
and gave awe in its place.

Communion

On the trail around Gordon's Pond,
Sunday morning,
hands held as if to receive the Eucharist
as I approached the rail,
the songs of the Marsh Wren and Red-Winged Blackbird,
the fragrance of pine and service berry
threaded through the scent of salt air and brackish water
were holy wafer and wine.

Notes Not Yet Sounded

Nine grandkids!
Today at eight to twenty-five,
they are my gift to the universe,
boisterous, bold, debating with each other and the stars
about what's important, believable, true.
They play games and sit in quiet corners to read a thousand books.
One still sleeps with a blanket for comfort,
two are gay, and three or more like to cook.
They eat, some for pleasure with chocolate syrup,
one vegetarian with restraint.
They are runners, swimmers, hikers, beer drinkers, and dreamers,
and I hear the perfect pitch of piano, cello, and trombone
even when the notes have not yet sounded.
They will.
These gifted ordinary human beings
have a song of life and hope and possibility
that make this a living day.

A poem excerpted from *lost and found, and other poems of loss, grief and joy*, Mary's first collection of poems, published in 2018.

Peaches

The peaches were on Anne's kitchen table
which had been covered with last week's Sunday paper,
and the sight of their luscious colors,
red, maroon, and orangey yellow
drew me to their fragrance,
I bent over to be close to them,
there must have been fifty,
waiting quietly to be touched,
gently.

"I've been waiting for them to be just right
for jam and canning and one peach pie.
I think they might be ready today."

What gave her hand the wisdom
to touch the peach and know today was the time,
to be able to declare this peach,
these peaches, have waited long enough,
the blossoms of spring have fulfilled their promise?

Waiting.
I wait for some wise hand to touch me,
to declare it is my time,
that I have ripened
and am enough.

www.ingramcontent.com/pod-product-compliance
Lightning Source LLC
Chambersburg PA
CBHW020950090426
42736CB00010B/1354